AIR FRYER COOKBOOK
FOR BEGINNERS
ON A BUDGET

CONTENTS

CONTENTS

Garrison's Of Potatoes with Chard and Cheese

Prep Time:

Cooking Time:

Servings:

Ingredients:

- 4 potatoes
- Swiss chard leaves
- 100ml milk cream
- 150g Gruyere grated cheese
- 1 garlic, mashed
- Olive oil
- Nutmeg
- Salt and pepper

Directions:

1. In a pot of water cook the potatoes for 20 minutes. Meanwhile, in a pot of boiling water place the chard for 1 minute, drain, cut finely and set aside. Cut into 2 the potatoes and remove the pulp without damaging the skin. Brown the garlic in oil, add chard, potato pulp, cream, walnut, salt and pepper and mix. Fill potatoes, sprinkle cheese and bring to Air Fryer at 180°C for 5 10 minutes. Serve up hot.

Spinach Eggs and Cheese

Prep Time: 20 min **Cooking Time:** 20 min **Servings:** 2

Ingredients:

- 3 whole eggs
- 3 oz cottage cheese
- 3-4 oz chopped spinach
- ¼ cup parmesan cheese
- ¼ cup of milk

Directions:

1. Preheat your fryer to 375°F/190°C.
2. In a large bowl, whisk the eggs, cottage cheese, the parmesan and the milk.
3. Mix in the spinach.
4. Transfer to a small, greased, fryer dish.
5. Sprinkle the cheese on top.
6. Bake for 25-30 minutes.
7. Let cool for 5 minutes and serve.

Bistro Wedges

Prep Time: 10 min   **Cooking Time:** 10 min   **Servings:** 4

Ingredients:

- 1 lb. fingerling potatoes, cut into wedges
- 1 tsp. extra virgin olive oil
- ½ tsp. garlic powder
- Salt and pepper to taste
- ½ cup raw cashews, soaked in water overnight
- ½ tsp. ground turmeric
- ½ tsp. paprika
- 1 tbsp. nutritional yeast
- 1 tsp. fresh lemon juice
- 2 tbsp. to ¼ cup water

Directions:

1. Pre-heat your Air Fryer at 400°F.
2. In a bowl, toss together the potato wedges, olive oil, garlic powder, and salt and pepper, making sure to coat the potatoes well.
3. Transfer the potatoes to the basket of your fryer and fry for 10 minutes.
4. In the meantime, prepare the cheese sauce. Pulse the cashews, turmeric, paprika, nutritional yeast, lemon juice, and water together in a food processor. Add more water to achieve your desired consistency.
5. When the potatoes are finished cooking, move them to a bowl that is small enough to fit inside the fryer and add the cheese sauce on top. Cook for an additional 3 minutes.

Toasted Cheese

Prep Time: 10 min   **Cooking Time:** 10 min   **Servings:** 2

Ingredients:

- 2 slices bread
- 4 oz cheese, grated
- Small amount of butter

Directions:

1. Grill the bread in the toaster.
2. Butter the toast and top with the grated cheese.
3. Set your Air Fryer to 350°F and allow to warm.
4. Put the toast slices inside the fryer and cook for 4 - 6 minutes.
5. Serve and enjoy!

Pea Delight

Prep Time: 13 min   **Cooking Time:** 12 min   **Servings:** 2-4

Ingredients:

- 1 cup flour
- 1 tsp. baking powder
- 3 eggs
- 1 cup coconut milk
- 1 cup cream cheese
- 3 tbsp. pea protein
- ½ cup chicken/turkey strips
- 1 pinch sea salt
- 1 cup mozzarella cheese

Directions:

1. Set your Air Fryer at 390°F and allow to warm.
2. In a large bowl, mix all ingredients together using a large wooden spoon.
3. Spoon equal amounts of the mixture into muffin cups and allow to cook for 15 minutes.

Toasties

Prep Time: 15 min   **Cooking Time:** 15 min   **Servings:** 2

Ingredients:

- ¼ cup milk or cream
- 2 sausages, boiled
- 3 eggs
- 1 slice bread, sliced lengthwise
- 4 tbsp. cheese, grated
- Sea salt to taste
- Chopped fresh herbs and steamed broccoli [optional]

Directions:

1. Pre-heat your Air Fryer at 360°F and set the timer for 5 minutes.

2. In the meantime, scramble the eggs in a bowl and add in the milk.

3. Grease three muffin cups with a cooking spray. Divide the egg mixture in three and pour equal amounts into each cup.

4. Slice the sausages and drop them, along with the slices of bread, into the egg mixture. Add the cheese on top and a little salt as desired.

5. Transfer the cups to the Fryer and cook for 15-20 minutes, depending on how firm you would like them. When ready, remove them from the fryer and serve with fresh herbs and steam broccoli if you prefer.

English Builder's Breakfast

Prep Time: 18 min   **Cooking Time:** 17 min   **Servings:** 2

Ingredients:

- 1 cup potatoes, sliced and diced
- 2 cups beans in tomato sauce
- 2 eggs
- 1 tbsp. olive oil
- 1 sausage
- Salt to taste

Directions:

1. Set your Air Fryer at 390°F and allow to warm.
2. Break the eggs onto an fryer-safe dish and sprinkle on some salt.
3. Lay the beans on the dish, next to the eggs.
4. In a bowl small enough to fit inside your fryer, coat the potatoes with the olive oil. Sprinkle on the salt, as desired.
5. Transfer the bowl of potato slices to the fryer and cook for 10 minutes.
6. Swap out the bowl of potatoes for the dish containing the eggs and beans. Leave to cook for another 10 minutes. Cover the potatoes with parchment paper.
7. Slice up the sausage and throw the slices in on top of the beans and eggs. Resume cooking for another 5 minutes. Serve with the potatoes, as well as toast and coffee if desired.

Taco Wraps

Prep Time: 15 min   **Cooking Time:** 15 min   **Servings:** 4

Ingredients:

- 1 tbsp. water
- 4 pc commercial vegan nuggets, chopped
- 1 small yellow onion, diced
- 1 small red bell pepper, chopped
- 2 cobs grilled corn kernels
- 4 large corn tortillas
- Mixed greens for garnish

Directions:

1. Pre-heat your Air Fryer at 400°F.

2. Over a medium heat, water-sauté the nuggets with the onions, corn kernels and bell peppers in a skillet, then remove from the heat.

3. Fill the tortillas with the nuggets and vegetables and fold them up. Transfer to the inside of the fryer and cook for 15 minutes. Once crispy, serve immediately, garnished with the mixed greens.

Filleting Of Strudel

Prep Time:

Cooking Time:

Servings:

Ingredients:

- 2 Washed potatoes
- 1 Washed eggplant
- Dry Thyme
- Salt
- Olive oil

Directions:

1. Cut into thin slices the potatoes and eggplant. Reserve up the potatoes in water and the eggplant sprinkle salt and place on absorbent paper. Prepare the mold of the Air Fryer with wax paper. Cover the base with potatoes, varnish with oil, sprinkle with salt and thyme. Add a layer of eggplant, varnish with oil and sprinkle with salt and thyme. Repeat until finishing the materials. Set the Air Fryer at 180°c for 25 30 minutes. Cut into 4, sprinkle with thyme and set at 200°c for 3 5 minutes.

2. Serve up immediately

Cannelloni In Tomato Sauce

Prep Time:

Cooking Time:

Servings:

Ingredients:

- 300g of lasagna pasta
- 400g of tomato
- 1 lemon
- Salt, sugar, and pepper
- Olive oil.
- 150g of spinach
- 250g ricotta cheese
- 8 cherry tomatoes
- 50g of Emmental cheese

Directions:

1. Prepare the spaghetti according to the manufacturer's instructions. Drain and bathe with ice water to cut the cooking. Process the tomatoes and place them in a mold, season, add a pinch of salt and a little sugar. Bring them to the fire until it is thick. Mix apart; ricotta, lemon juice, spinach and salt pepper. Fill the dough and close them like a cylinder. They are placed in the mold of the Air Fryer with sauce in the bottom. They bathe with sauce and sprinkle with Emmental cheese. It is programmed for 812 minutes at 180 °C.

2. Serve up hot.

Bread Rolls

Prep Time: 15 min   **Cooking Time:** 15 min   **Servings:** 5

Ingredients:

- 5 large potatoes, boiled and mashed
- Salt and pepper to taste
- 1 tbsp. olive oil
- ½ tsp. mustard seeds
- 2 small onions, chopped
- ½ tsp. turmeric
- 2 sprigs curry leaves
- 8 slices of bread, brown sides discarded
- 2 green chilis, seeded and chopped
- 1 bunch coriander, chopped

Directions:

1. Pre-heat your Air Fryer at 400°F.

2. Put the mashed potatoes in a bowl and sprinkle on salt and pepper. Set to one side.

3. Fry the mustard seeds in a little olive oil over a medium-low heat, stirring continuously, until they sputter.

4. Add in the onions and cook until they turn translucent. Add the curry leaves and turmeric powder and stir. Cook for a further 2 minutes until fragrant.

5. Remove the pan from the heat and combine the contents with the potatoes. Remove from heat and add to the potatoes. Mix in the green chilies and coriander.

6. Wet the bread slightly and drain of any excess liquid.

7. Spoon a small amount of the potato mixture into the center of the bread and enclose the bread around the filling, sealing it entirely. Continue until the rest of the bread and filling is used up. Brush each bread roll with some oil and transfer to the basket of your fryer.

8. Cook for 15 minutes, gently shaking the fryer basket at the halfway point to ensure each roll is cooked evenly.

Peanut Butter Bread

Prep Time: 8 min   **Cooking Tim:** 7 min   **Servings:** 3

Ingredients:

- 1 tbsp. oil
- 2 tbsp. peanut butter
- 4 slices bread
- 1 banana, sliced

Directions:

1. Spread the peanut butter on top of each slice of bread, then arrange the banana slices on top. Sandwich two slices together, then the other two.

2. Oil the inside of the Air Fryer and cook the bread for 5 minutes at 300°F.

Egg Muffin Sandwich

Prep Time: 8 min   **Cooking Time:** 7 min   **Servings:** 1

Ingredients:

- 1 egg
- 2 slices bacon
- 1 English muffin

Directions:

1. Pre-heat your Air Fryer at 395°F

2. Take a ramekin and spritz it with cooking spray. Break an egg into the ramekin before transferring it to the basket of your fryer, along with the English muffin and bacon slices, keeping each component separate.

3. Allow to cook for 6 minutes. After removing from the fryer, allow to cool for around two minutes. Halve the muffin.

4. Create your sandwich by arranging the egg and bacon slices on the base and topping with the other half of the muffin.

Cheddar & Bacon Quiche

Prep Time: 15 min   **Cooking Time:** 15 min   **Servings:** 4

Ingredients:

- 3 tbsp. Greek yogurt
- ½ cup grated cheddar cheese
- 3 oz. chopped bacon
- 4 eggs, beaten
- ¼ tsp. garlic powder
- Pinch of black pepper
- 1 shortcrust pastry
- ¼ tsp. onion powder
- ¼ tsp. sea salt
- Some flour for sprinkling

Directions:

1. Pre-heat your Air Fryer at 330°F.

2. Take 8 ramekins and grease with a little oil. Coat with a sprinkling of flour, tapping to remove any excess.

3. Cut the shortcrust pastry in 8 and place each piece at the bottom of each ramekin.

4. Put all of the other ingredients in a bowl and combine well. Spoon equal amounts of the filling into each piece of pastry.

5. Cook the ramekins in the Air Fryer for 20 minutes.

Black's Bangin' Casserole

Prep Time: 20 min   **Cooking Time:** 20 min   **Servings:** 4

Ingredients:

- 5 eggs
- 3 tbsp chunky tomato sauce
- 2 tbsp heavy cream
- 2 tbsp grated parmesan cheese

Directions:

1. Preheat your fryer to 350°F/175°C.
2. Combine the eggs and cream in a bowl.
3. Mix in the tomato sauce and add the cheese.
4. Spread into a glass baking dish and bake for 25-35 minutes.
5. Top with extra cheese.
6. Enjoy!

Veg Frittata

Prep Time: 18 min **Cooking Time:** 17 min **Servings:** 2

Ingredients:

- ¼ cup milk
- 1 zucchini
- ½ bunch asparagus
- ½ cup mushrooms
- ½ cup spinach or baby spinach
- ½ cup red onion, sliced
- 4 eggs
- ½ tbsp. olive oil
- 5 tbsp. feta cheese, crumbled
- 4 tbsp. cheddar, grated
- ¼ bunch chives, minced
- Sea salt and pepper to taste

Directions:

1. In a bowl, mix together the eggs, milk, salt and pepper.

2. Cut up the zucchini, asparagus, mushrooms and red onion into slices. Shred the spinach using your hands.

3. Over a medium heat, stir-fry the vegetables for 5 – 7 minutes with the olive oil in a non-stick pan.

4. Place some parchment paper in the base of a baking tin. Pour in the vegetables, followed by the egg mixture. Top with the feta and grated cheddar.

5. Set the Air Fryer at 320°F and allow to warm for five minutes.

6. Transfer the baking tin to the fryer and allow to cook for 15 minutes. Take care when removing the frittata from the Air Fryer and leave to cool for 5 minutes.

7. Top with the minced chives and serve.

Tomatoes 3 Textures with Macaroni

Prep Time:

Cooking Time:

Servings:

Ingredients:

- 500g macaroni
- 1 garlic, mashed
- 1 onion
- 300g tomato
- 200ml vegetable broth
- 8 dried tomatoes in julienne
- 10 cherry tomatoes sliced in 4
- 150g grated cheese
- 15g butter
- Sugar, salt, pepper, and oregano

Directions:

1. In a pot with water, place garlic, onion, and tomato to boil for 30 minutes. Process in a blender and bring once more to a boil. Add salt, pepper, and sugar. Add broth, dry tomatoes and boil until homogenized. Make the macaroni to taste and place them in the mold of the Air Fryer incorporating well. Add oregano, cheese, cherry tomatoes and set at 180°c for 10 15 minutes.

2. Serve up hot

Cinnamon Toasts

Prep Time: 8 min   **Cooking Time:** 7 min   **Servings:** 4

Ingredients:

- 10 bread slices
- 1 pack salted butter
- 4 tbsp. sugar
- 2 tsp. ground cinnamon
- ½ tsp. vanilla extract

Directions:

1. In a bowl, combine the butter, cinnamon, sugar, and vanilla extract. Spread onto the slices of bread.

2. Set your Air Fryer to 380°F. When warmed up, put the bread inside the fryer and cook for 4 – 5 minutes.

Cheese & Chicken Sandwich

Prep Time: 8 min   **Cooking Time:** 7 min   **Servings:** 1

Ingredients:

- 1/3 cup chicken, cooked and shredded
- 2 mozzarella slices
- 1 hamburger bun
- ¼ cup cabbage, shredded
- 1 tsp. mayonnaise
- 2 tsp. butter
- 1 tsp. olive oil
- ½ tsp. balsamic vinegar
- 1/4 tsp. smoked paprika
- ¼ tsp. black pepper
- ¼ tsp. garlic powder
- Pinch of salt

Directions:

1. Pre-heat your Air Fryer at 370°F.
2. Apply some butter to the outside of the hamburger bun with a brush.
3. In a bowl, coat the chicken with the garlic powder, salt, pepper, and paprika.
4. In a separate bowl, stir together the mayonnaise, olive oil, cabbage, and balsamic vinegar to make coleslaw.
5. Slice the bun in two. Start building the sandwich, starting with the chicken, followed by the mozzarella, the coleslaw, and finally the top bun.
6. Transfer the sandwich to the fryer and cook for 5 – 7 minutes.

French Toast

Prep Time: 13 min   **Cooking Time:** 12 min   **Servings:** 2

Ingredients:

- 4 slices bread of your choosing
- 2 tbsp. soft butter
- 2 eggs, lightly beaten
- Pinch of salt
- Pinch of cinnamon
- Pinch of ground nutmeg
- Pinch of ground cloves
- Nonstick cooking spray
- Sugar for serving

Directions:

1. In a shallow bowl, mix together the salt, spices and eggs.

2. Butter each side of the slices of bread and slice into strips. You may also use cookie cutters for this step.

3. Set your Air Fryer to 350°F and allow to warm up briefly.

.4. Dredge each strip of bread in the egg and transfer to the fryer. Cook for two minutes, ensuring the toast turns golden brown.

5. At this point, spritz the tops of the bread strips with cooking spray, flip, and cook for another 4 minutes on the other side. Top with a light dusting of sugar before serving.

Gratin with Herbs with Provolone

Prep Time:

Cooking Time:

Servings:

Ingredients:

- 2 potatoes
- 300ml milk cream
- 1 garlic, mashed
- Rosemary, Laurel
- Salt and pepper
- Spicy and sweet paprika
- 100g provolone cheese
- 2 tablespoons breadcrumbs
- Pepper in grains
- Olive oil

Directions:

1. Cut the potatoes into thin slices and Reserve up in the water. Bring a pot with milk, garlic, rosemary, and pepper in grains and bay leaf to the fire. Stir gently until it boils and reduces the heat. Leave to aromatize for 10 minutes. Add salt and sweet and spicy paprika. Drain and dry the potatoes Coat the Air Fryer mold with oil and place the potatoes in layers, seasoning each one. Strain the milk sauce and pour over the potatoes. Cover with aluminum foil and program it at 180ºc for 25 30 minutes. Remove the aluminum, sprinkle cheese and program for 8 15 minutes.

2. Serve up hot.

Chia & Oat Porridge

Prep Time: 8 min   **Cooking Time:** 7 min   **Servings:** 4

Ingredients:

- 4 cups milk
- 2 tbsp. peanut butter
- 2 cups oats
- 1 cup chia seeds
- 4 tbsp. honey
- 1 tbsp. butter, melted

Directions:

1. Pre-heat the Air Fryer to 390°F.

2. Put the peanut butter, honey, butter, and milk in a bowl and mix together using a whisk. Add in the oats and chia seeds and stir.

3. Transfer the mixture to an fryer-proof bowl that is small enough to fit inside the fryer and cook for 5 minutes. Give another stir before serving.

Rice Paper Bacon

Prep Time: 15 min   **Cooking Time:** 15 min   **Servings:** 4

Ingredients:

- 3 tbsp. soy sauce or tamari
- 2 tbsp. cashew butter
- 2 tbsp. liquid smoke
- 2 tbsp. water
- 4 pc white rice paper, cut into 1-inch thick strips

Directions:

1. Pre-heat your Air Fryer at 350°F.
2. Mix together the soy sauce/tamari, liquid smoke, water, and cashew butter in a large bowl.
3. Take the strips of rice paper and soak them for 5 minutes. Arrange in one layer in the bottom of your fryer.
4. Cook for 15 minutes, ensuring they become crispy, before serving with some vegetables.

Posh Soufflé

Prep Time: 13 min   **Cooking Time:** 12 min   **Servings:** 4

Ingredients:

- ¼ cup flour
- 1/3 cup butter
- 1 cup milk
- 4 egg yolks
- 1 tsp. vanilla extract
- 6 egg whites
- 1 oz. sugar
- 1 tsp. cream of tartar

Directions:

1. Set your Air Fryer at 320°F and allow to warm.

2. In a bowl, mix together the butter and flour until a smooth consistency is achieved.

3. Pour the milk into a saucepan over a low-to-medium heat. Add in the and allow to dissolve before raising the heat to boil the milk.

4. Pour in the flour and butter mixture and stir rigorously for 7 minutes to eliminate any lumps. Make sure the mixture thickens. Take off the heat and allow to cool for 15 minutes.

5. Spritz 6 soufflé dishes with oil spray.

6. Place the egg yolks and vanilla extract in a separate bowl and beat them together with a fork. Pour in the milk and combine well to incorporate everything.

7. In a smaller bowl mix together the egg whites and cream of tartar with a fork. Fold into the egg yolks-milk mixture before adding in the flour mixture. Transfer equal amounts to the 6 soufflé dishes.

8. Put the dishes in the fryer and cook for 15 minutes.

Bacon & Horseradish Cream

Prep Time: 50 min   **Cooking Time:** 50 min   **Servings:** 4

Ingredients:

- ½ lb. thick cut bacon, diced
- 2 tbsp. butter
- 2 shallots, sliced
- ½ cup milk
- 1 ½ lb. Brussels sprouts, halved
- 2 tbsp. flour
- 1 cup heavy cream
- 2 tbsp. prepared horseradish
- ½ tbsp. fresh thyme leaves
- 1/8 tsp. ground nutmeg
- 1 tbsp. olive oil
- ½ tsp. sea salt
- Ground black pepper to taste
- ½ cup water

Directions:

Pre-heat your Air Fryer at 400°F.

Coat the Brussels sprouts with olive oil and sprinkle some salt and pepper on top. Transfer to the fryer and cook for a half hour. At the halfway point, give them a good stir, then take them out of the fryer and set to the side.

Put the bacon in the basket of the fryer and pour the water into the drawer underneath to catch the fat. Cook for 10 minutes, stirring 2 or 3 times throughout the cooking time.

When 10 minutes are up, add in the shallots. Cook for a further 10 – 15 minutes, making sure the shallots soften up and the bacon turns brown. Add some more pepper and remove. Leave to drain on some paper towels.

Melt the butter over the stove or in the microwave, before adding in the flour and mixing with a whisk. Slowly add in the heavy cream and milk, and continue to whisk for another 3 – 5 minutes, making sure the mixture thickens.

Add the horseradish, thyme, salt, and nutmeg and stirring well once more.

Take a 9" x 13" baking dish and grease it with oil. Pre-heat your fryer to 350°F.

Put the Brussels sprouts in the baking dish and spread them across the base. Pour over the cream sauce and then top with a layer of bacon and shallots.

Cook in the fryer for a half hour and enjoy.

Rice with Pepper

Prep Time:

Cooking Time:

Servings:

Ingredients:

- ½ purple onion finely cut
- Olive oil
- 1 garlic, mashed
- 3 julienne peppers (red, yellow and green)
- 2 cups of rice
- 1L hot vegetable broth
- Salt and pepper

Directions:

1. Sauté the onion with garlic and paprika. Add rice and sauté. Take everything to the mold of the Air Fryer and pour the broth. Season, mix, cover with aluminum foil and program it at 180°C for 25 30 minutes. When cooking, remove the aluminum. Let stand for 5 minutes and Serve up

American Donuts

Prep Time: 40 min   **Cooking Time:** 40 min   **Servings:** 6

Ingredients:

- 1 cup flour
- ¼ cup sugar
- 1 tsp. baking powder
- ½ tsp. salt
- ¼ tsp. cinnamon
- 1 tbsp. coconut oil, melted
- 2 tbsp. aquafaba or liquid from canned chickpeas
- ¼ cup milk

Directions:

1. Put the sugar, flour and baking powder in a bowl and combine. Mix in the salt and cinnamon.
2. In a separate bowl, combine the aquafaba, milk and coconut oil.
3. Slowly pour the dry ingredients into the wet ingredients and combine well to create a sticky dough.
4. Refrigerate for at least an hour.
5. Pre-heat your Air Fryer at 370°F.
6. Using your hands, shape the dough into several small balls and place each one inside the fryer. Cook for 10 minutes, refraining from shaking the basket as they cook.
7. Lightly dust the balls with sugar and cinnamon and serve with a hot cup of coffee.

Choco Bars

Prep Time: 15 min   **Cooking Time:** 15 min   **Servings:** 8

Ingredients:

- 2 cups old-fashioned oats
- ½ cup quinoa, cooked
- ½ cup chia seeds
- ½ cup s, sliced
- ½ cup dried cherries, chopped
- ½ cup dark chocolate, chopped
- ¾ cup butter
- 1/3 cup honey
- 2 tbsp. coconut oil
- ¼ tsp. salt
- ½ cup prunes, pureed

Directions:

1. Pre-heat your Air Fryer at 375°F.
2. Put the oats, quinoa, s, cherries, chia seeds, and chocolate in a bowl and mix well.
3. Heat the butter, honey, and coconut oil in a saucepan, gently stirring together. Pour this over the oats mixture.
4. Mix in the salt and pureed prunes and combine well.
5. Transfer this to a baking dish small enough to fit inside the fryer and cook for 15 minutes. Remove from the fryer and allow to cool completely. Cut into bars and enjoy.

Papillote Of Feta Cheese with Vegetables

Prep Time:

Cooking Time:

Servings:

Ingredients:

- Feta cheese
- 100g onion julienne
- 200g julienne paprika
- Dried oregano
- Garlic powder
- Salt and pepper
- Olive oil

Directions:

1. Cut 2 rectangles of aluminum foil, place onion and pa prika. On these the cheese, sprinkle with oregano, garlic and salt pepper, cover with the other rectangle and seal the edges. Bring the Air Fryer to 180°C for 12 18 minutes. Carefully open the envelope,

2. Serve up hot bathing with oil.

Golden Cauliflower

Prep Time:

Cooking Time:

Servings:

Ingredients:

- ½ defrosted cauliflower
- Salt and pepper
- Paprika
- Turmeric
- ½ teaspoon of cayenne
- 1 teaspoon of sugar
- Olive oil
- 1 garlic, mashed

Directions:

1. In a pot of boiling water, cook cauliflower for 1 minute. Drain and Reserve. In a bowl mix the rest of Ingredients until well integrated. Add the cauliflower and completely impregnate. Take the Air Fryer programmed at 180°c for 15 25 minutes and

2. Serve up hot

Laurel Joys

Prep Time:

Cooking Time:

Servings:

Ingredients:

- 1 ½ kg of small parboiled potatoes.
- 12 bay leaves.
- 5 tablespoons of olive oil.
- 2 cloves of garlic
- Coarse salt.
- Pepper.

Directions:

1. Open a hole to the potatoes in the center and insert a bay leaf. Place in a deep dish, oil, and garlic cloves. They are taken to the Air Fryer for 5 minutes at 180°c. Add the potatoes and set the Air Fryer to 180 °c, for 2025 minutes, interrupt the cooking and turn the potatoes, re move and continue.

2. Place salt and pepper to taste, and spices to taste.

Chorizo Risotto

Prep Time: 40 min   **Cooking Time:** 40 min   **Servings:** 4

Ingredients:

- ¼ cup milk
- ½ cup flour
- 4 oz. breadcrumbs
- 4 oz. chorizo, finely sliced
- 1 serving mushroom risotto rice
- 1 egg
- Sea salt to taste

Directions:

1. In a bowl, combine the mushroom risotto rice with the risotto and salt before refrigerating to cool.

2. Set your Air Fryer at 390°F and leave to warm for 5 minutes.

3. Use your hands to form 2 tablespoonfuls of risotto into a rice ball. Repeat until you have used up all the risotto. Roll each ball in the flour.

4. Crack the egg into a bowl and mix with the milk using a whisk. Coat each rice ball in the egg-milk mixture, and then in breadcrumbs.

5. Space the rice balls out in the baking dish of the Air Fryer. Bake for 20 minutes, ensuring they develop a crispy golden-brown crust.

6. Serve warm with a side of fresh vegetables and salad if desired.

Spinach Balls

Prep Time: 10 min   **Cooking Time:** 10 min   **Servings:** 4

Ingredients:

- 1 carrot, peeled and grated
- 1 package fresh spinach, blanched and chopped
- ½ onion, chopped
- 1 egg, beaten
- ½ tsp. garlic powder
- 1 tsp. garlic, minced
- 1 tsp. salt
- ½ tsp. black pepper
- 1 tbsp. nutritional yeast
- 1 tbsp. flour
- 2 slices bread, toasted

Directions:

1. In a food processor, pulse the toasted bread to form breadcrumbs. Transfer into a shallow dish or bowl.
2. In a bowl, mix together all the other ingredients.
3. Use your hands to shape the mixture into small-sized balls. Roll the balls in the breadcrumbs, ensuring to cover them well.
4. Put in the Air Fryer and cook at 390°F for 10 minutes.

Tofu Scramble

Prep Time: 20 min   **Cooking Time:** 20 min   **Servings:** 3

Ingredients:

- 2 ½ cups red potato, chopped
- 1 tbsp. olive oil
- 1 block tofu, chopped finely
- 1tbsp. olive oil
- 2 tbsp. tamari
- 1 tsp. turmeric powder
- ½ tsp. onion powder
- ½ tsp. garlic powder
- ½ cup onion, chopped
- 4 cups broccoli florets

Directions:

1. Pre-heat the Air Fryer at 400°F.
2. Toss together the potatoes and olive oil.
3. Cook the potatoes in a baking dish for 15 minutes, shaking once during the cooking time to ensure they fry evenly.
4. Combine the tofu, olive oil, turmeric, onion powder, tamari, and garlic powder together, before stirring in the onions, followed by the broccoli.
5. Top the potatoes with the tofu mixture and allow to cook for an additional 15 minutes. Serve warm.

Avocado Tempura

Prep Time: 10 min **Cooking Time:** 10 min **Servings:** 4

Ingredients:

- ½ cup breadcrumbs
- ½ tsp. salt
- 1 Haas avocado, pitted, peeled and sliced
- Liquid from 1 can white beans or aquafaba

Directions:

1. Set your Air Fryer to 350°F and allow to warm.

2. Mix the breadcrumbs and salt in a shallow bowl until well-incorporated.

3. Dip the avocado slices in the bean/aquafaba juice, then into the breadcrumbs. Put the avocados in the fryer, taking care not to overlap any slices, and fry for 10 minutes, giving the basket a good shake at the halfway point.

Roasted Potatoes with Paprika

Prep Time:

Cooking Time:

Servings:

Ingredients:

- 2kg of potatoes parboiled in squares.
- 60 gr of toasted breadcrumbs.
- 1/2 teaspoons of paprika
- 10 teaspoons of oil.
- Salt

Directions:

1. Mix the potatoes with the Breadcrumbs, paprika, salt and 3 tablespoons of oil. Place a little oil on a baking sheet, when the oil is hot, add the potato mixture, and place some Breadcrumbs on top. Bring the Air Fryer to a temperature of 180°c, for 2530 minutes stirring occasionally, check the cooking and repeat the cycle if necessary.

2. The potatoes should be golden brown.

Coriander and Parsley Mojito

Prep Time:

Cooking Time:

Servings:

Ingredients:

- 1 cup of olive oil
- ½ cup of coriander leaves
- ½ cups of parsley
- 1 chopped onion
- 2 chopped garlic
- Salt and pepper
- 2 tablespoons of mustard.
- Olive oil

Directions:

1. In the Air Fryer mold, place oil and set at 180°c for 5 minutes. Place onion, garlic, and stir. Set at 140°c for 5 8 minutes. Bring to the blender and process with the rest of the Ingredients .

2. Allow to cool and Reserve up in the refrigerator.

Roasted Vegetables with Cheese

Prep Time:

Cooking Time:

Servings:

Ingredients:

- ¼Kg cheese in cubes
- 3 peppers in squares (yellow, green and red)
- 1 pumpkin in sheets
- 6 mushrooms in quarters
- 2 garlic
- Olive oil
- Salt and pepper

Directions:

1. Add all the Ingredients to the Air Fryer, bathe with oil and mix. Season and program it at 180°C for 10 15 minutes stirring periodically.

2. Serve up as a side dish.

Eggs with Arrabiata

Prep Time:

Cooking Time:

Servings:

Ingredients:

- 4 eggs
- 4 tomatoes
- 4 tablespoons fried tomato
- 1 paprika
- 1 rolled garlic
- Oregano
- Chili

Directions:

1. Finely cut tomato, paprika, and chili pepper. Sauté the garlic in oil until it changes color and adds tomato, al lowing it to cook while stirring. Add paprika without stirring. Add the chili, mix and finish with fried tomato. Once it reaches the boil, add it to the fire and place it in the mold of the Air Fryer. Add the eggs and set at 180°c for 7 12 minutes.

2. Serve up hot.

CheeseCream

Prep Time:

Cooking Time:

Servings:

Ingredients:

- ½ finely cut onion
- Olive oil
- 1 garlic, mashed
- 500g cheese in small cubes
- 1L vegetable broth
- Salt and pepper

Directions:

1. Sauté the onion until browned, add garlic and cheese while stirring. Process in a blender with salt and pepper broth. Take the mold of the Air Fryer programming at 180°C for 25 30 minutes.

2. Serve up hot.

Poblano's Pasta with Cheese

Prep Time:

Cooking Time:

Servings:

Ingredients:

- 1 garlic, mashed
- ¼ finely chopped onion
- Butter
- 2 roasted and peeled poblano peppers
- 2 cups of chicken broth
- 3 tablespoons of milk cream
- Salt and pepper
- 600g fettuccine
- 250g cubed cheese in cubes

Directions:

1. Sauté the garlic, onion, chilies and mix well. Process the sauté with broth and cream. Season and bring to the mold of the Air Fryer programmed at 180°C for 20 25 minutes. Cook the pasta to taste. Missing 5 minutes add pasta and cheese. Finish programming and

2. Serve up hot.

Puff Pastry with Vegetables

Prep Time:

Cooking Time:

Servings:

Ingredients:

- 1 sheet of puff pastry
- 1 zucchini in half moon
- 2 crescent tomatoes
- 1 julienne onion
- olive oil
- grated mozzarella
- salt and pepper

Directions:

1. Cut the puff pastry into 4 portions, puncture each portion and bring to a tray suitable for the Air Fryer. Place cheese, onion, zucchini, and tomato. Season and bathe with oil. Take the Air Fryer programmed at 180°C for 15
2. 20 minutes. Let cool and Serve up.

Carrot Omelet In A Blender

Prep Time:

Cooking Time:

Servings:

Ingredients:

- 6 eggs
- 750g chopped carrots
- Olive oil
- Salt, pepper, and oregano

Directions:

1. In the blender add the eggs, add the carrots little by little and process. Add oil to the Air Fryer mold and program it at 180°C for 5 minutes. Add the mixture and program it at 180°C for 8 12 minutes.

2. Serve up hot

Spinach Quiche

Prep Time: 40 min   **Cooking Time:** 35 min   **Servings:** 4

Ingredients:

- ¾ cup flour
- Pinch of salt
- ½ cup cold coconut oil
- 2 tbsp. cold water
- 2 tbsp. olive oil
- 1 onion, chopped
- 4 oz. mushrooms, sliced
- 1 package firm tofu, pressed to remove excess water, then crumbled
- 1 lb. spinach, washed and chopped
- ½ tbsp. dried dill
- 2 tbsp. nutritional yeast
- Salt and pepper
- Sprig of fresh parsley, chopped

Directions:

1. Pre-heat the Air Fryer at 375°F.

2. Firstly, prepare the pastry. Use a sieve to sift together the salt and flour into a bowl. Combine with the coconut oil to make the flour crumbly. Slowly pour in the water until a stiff dough is formed.

3. Wrap the dough in saran wrap and refrigerate for a half hour.

4. Sauté the onion in a skillet over medium heat for a minute. Add in the tofu and mushroom, followed by the spinach, yeast, and dill.

5. Sprinkle in salt and pepper as desired. Finally add in the parsley. Take the skillet off the heat.

6. Dust a flat surface with flour and roll out the dough until it is thin.

7. Grease a baking dish that is small enough to fit inside the fryer. Place the dough in the tin and pour in the tofu mixture. Transfer the dish to the fryer and cook for 30 minutes, ensuring the pastry crisps up.

Avocado Eggs

Prep Time: 8 min   **Cooking Time:** 7 min   **Servings:** 4

Ingredients:

- 2 large avocados, sliced
- 1 cup breadcrumbs
- ½ cup flour 2 eggs, beaten
- ¼ tsp. paprika
- Salt and pepper to taste

Directions:

1. Pre-heat your Air Fryer at 400°F for 5 minutes.

2. Sprinkle some salt and pepper on the slices of avocado. Optionally, you can enhance the flavor with a half-tsp. of dried oregano.

3. Lightly coat the avocados with flour. Dredge them in the eggs, before covering with breadcrumbs. Transfer to the fryer and cook for 6 minutes.

Bean Cream

Prep Time:

Cooking Time:

Servings:

Ingredients:

- 250g of beans
- Water
- ½ onion
- 1 garlic, mashed
- 2 leaves of holy grass
- ½L milk
- Olive oil
- Salt and pepper
- Grated cheese
- Corntortillas.

Directions:

1. In a pressure cooker place beans with water, onion, gar lic and holy herb leaves. When cooking, process everything with the broth and milk. Take to the mold of the Air Fryer and program it at 180°C for 25 30 minutes. Season and program for 15 20 minutes. Meanwhile, toast tortillas and cut into a strip.

2. Serve up the cream with cheese and tortillas

Rice and Chickpea Casserole

Prep Time:

Cooking Time:

Servings:

Ingredients:

- 240g long grain rice
- 2 kinds of garlic, mashed
- 1 finely cut purple onion
- 1 carrot, 1 paprika and 1 zucchini in small cubes
- 100g cooked chickpeas
- 1 teaspoon turmeric
- 1 teaspoon ground cumin
- 450ml vegetable broth
- Olive oil
- Salt and pepper

Directions:

1. Heat the broth until it boils. Sauté the onion and garlic over low heat. Add carrot, pepper and sauté for 10 minutes stirring. Finally, add zucchini and sauté for 5 more minutes. Add the rice, salt, pepper, cumin, turmeric and mix well to impregnate with oil. Place the rice in the mold of the Air Fryer and pour the broth. Mix and program it at 180°c for 15 20 minutes.

2. Cover with ab sorbent paper and let stand for 5 minutes until serving.

Cauliflower Stir Fry

Prep Time:

Cooking Time:

Servings:

Ingredients:

- 1 chopped cauliflower
- finely cut parsley
- 2 kinds of garlic, mashed
- 1 finely cut tomato
- olive oil
- paprika
- salt and pepper

Directions:

1. Bring the cauliflower to the Air Fryer mold, season and season with paprika. Schedule at 180°C for 10 15 minutes. Meanwhile, sauté parsley, garlic, and oil until browned. Add the tomato, salt, and pepper, mix and sauté for 5 minutes. Add the cauliflower and mix everything. Take everything to the Air Fryer mold and program for 8 12 minutes.

2. Serve up hot.

77

Romanesque Turkey

Prep Time:

Cooking Time:

Servings:

Ingredients:

- 1 turkey breast
- 1 tbsp lemon rind
- Sea salt
- 1 pinch of turmeric
- ½ cup of chimichurri
- 1 cup of mint leaves
- 1 cup of carrot paste
- Yellow lemon
- Olive oil
- 1 cooked celery

Directions:

1. Slice the turkey breasts, and season with the spices, place the lemon zest. Bring to the fryer and fry in the Air Fryer for 1225 minutes at 180°C. Halfway through the cooking turn around to cook on both sides. When ready, cut into pieces and Serve up with celery and lemon slices.

2. Garnish with the prepared sauce.

Chicken Fillets & Brie

Prep Time: 20 min   **Cooking Time:** 20 min   **Servings:** 4

Ingredients:

- 4 slices turkey, cured
- 2 large chicken fillets
- 4 slices brie cheese
- 1 tbsp. chives, chopped
- Salt and pepper to taste

Directions:

1. Pre-heat Air Fryer to 360°F. Slice each chicken fillet in half and sprinkle on salt and pepper. Coat with the brie and chives.

2. Wrap the turkey around the chicken and secure with toothpick.

3. Cook for 15 minutes until a brown color is achieved.

Caramelized Chicken Breasts

Prep Time:

Cooking Time:

Servings:

Ingredients:

- Olive oil
- Honey.
- Soy oil.
- Salt.
- Grated ginger.
- Oregano.
- Garlic.
- Pepper.
- Lemon juice.

Directions:

1. They are marinated for an hour the boned breasts and then drain. Fry in Air Fryer for 1015 minutes at 180ºC

2. It is served up with poached potatoes.

Italian Chicken Surprise

Prep Time:

Cooking Time:

Servings:

Ingredients:

- 4 cups of broccoli
- Sea salt for birds
- 2 cups of carrot paste
- 1 cup of chopped beans
- ¼ red paprika
- 4 fillets of chicken breasts
- Olive oil.

Directions:

1. Season the chicken breasts with sea salt for poultry and paprika. Place it, and fry in the Air Fryer for 815 minutes at 180°C. In a separate medium bowl, mix the broc coli, paprika, beans, carrot paste and salt to taste. Sauté the vegetables in olive oil. Serve up the breasts with the vegetables sautéed on top. Accompany it with rice, steamed potatoes, salads or whatever you like.

2. Decorate your taste.

Thyme Chicken

Prep Time:

Cooking Time:

Servings:

Ingredients:

- 1 chicken, chopped into small cubes
- 8 cloves of garlic cloves
- 1 lemon juice
- Thyme
- Salt and pepper to taste
- Olive oil

Directions:

1. Place the chicken in a bowl and salt and pepper. Add the garlic and lemon juice. Sprinkle with thyme and stir. Cover with plastic wrap and refrigerate for 2 hours. Place the chicken in the mold of the Air Fryer and sprin kle with olive oil. Mix and fry for 180°C for 10 15 minutes. Remove and check the chicken. Fry for 20 more minutes.

2. Serve up with rice or puree.

Flatbread

Prep Time: 10 min   **Cooking Time:** 10 min   **Servings:** 1

Ingredients:

- 1 cup mozzarella cheese, shredded
- ¼ cup blanched finely ground flour
- 1 oz. full-fat cream cheese, softened

Directions:

1. Microwave the mozzarella for half a minute until melted. Combine with the flour to achieve a smooth consistency, before adding the cream cheese. Keep mixing to create a dough, microwaving the mixture again if the cheese begins to harden.

2. Divide the dough into two equal pieces. Between two sheets of parchment paper, roll out the dough until it is about a quarter-inch thick. Cover the bottom of your fryer with another sheet of parchment.

3. Transfer the dough into the fryer and cook at 320°F for seven minutes. You may need to complete this step in two batches. Make sure to turn the flatbread halfway through cooking. Take care when removing it from the fryer and serve warm.

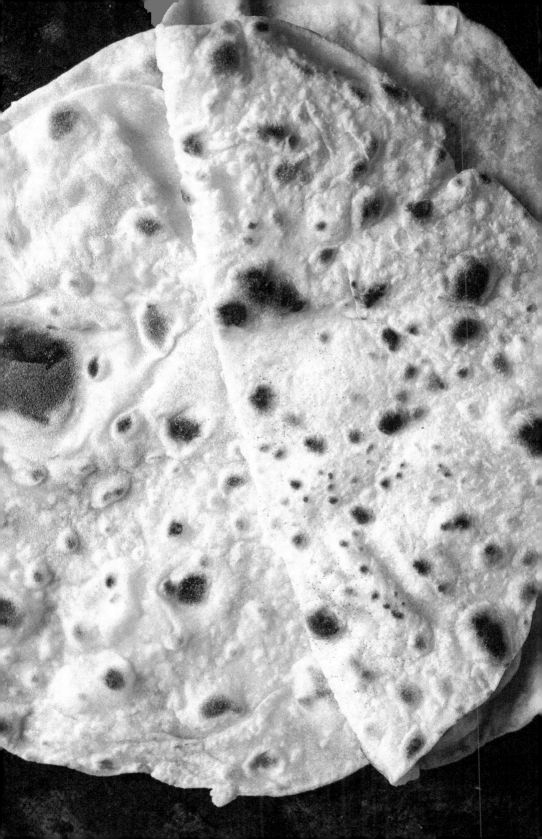

Chicken Pizza

Prep Time:

Cooking Time:

Servings:

Ingredients:

- 6 pita bread
- ½ Chicken breast cut into pieces
- 1 Fried Tomato Tin
- Black olives
- Oregano
- Grated cheese

Directions:

1. First, on each bread, place a layer of fried tomato. Add the cubed breast, olives, oregano and cheese. Fry in the Air Fryer at 160°C for 10 15 minutes.

2. They a Reserved up hot and full.

Chicken with Prunes

Prep Time:

Cooking Time:

Servings:

Ingredients:

- 4 thighs
- 1cda cumin
- 2 tbsp garlic
- 1 tbsp of oregano
- 1 cup chopped chives
- 3 red chili peppers
- 3 green chili
- 2 tbsp of ginger
- 2 tbsp of butter
- ½ cup flour
- Laurel
- 1 carrot in julienne
- 1 cup of chicken broth
- 1 cup of malt
- 1 cup of plums
- Garlic
- Salt
- English sauce
- Tomato paste
- Garlic
- Coriander

Directions:

1. The chicken pieces are seasoned. Pass through flour, sauté Air Fryer for 1522 minutes at 180°C. Flip the chicken halfway through the cycle to cook on the other side. Apart cooking is chopped onion and garlic chopped. Add chicken broth, soy sauce, and malt. Add the carrot, chili peppers, and a little broth. Add the plums and finally the chopped coriander.

2. The chicken is served up accompanied by the previous Preparation .

Baked Wings with Tartar

Prep Time:

Cooking Time:

Servings:

Ingredients:

- 24 Chicken wings
- 6 Cloves of garlic, mashed
- 2 Tbs. Of English sauce
- 4 Tbs. Of wheat flour
- 1 cup of breadcrumbs
- 2 beaten eggs
- Salt and pepper
- 1 cup of mayonnaise
- 1 tablespoon Of capers
- 2 Hard eggs
- 1 Cut onion
- 6 Gherkins in pickles
- 1 tablespoon Of parsley
- Parsley to decorate

Directions:

1. In a bowl add the wings. Add the garlic, English sauce and salt. Mix and Reserve up. While in the blender place the mayonnaise, capers, eggs, onion, pickles, parsley and process. Reserve up. Drain the wings and pass through wheat flour, beaten egg and Breadcrumbs. Place them in the Air Fryer and fry them at 180°C for 5 10 minutes.

2. Serve up them accompanied by tartar sauce.

Chicken Breasts with English Sauce and Lemon

Prep Time:

Cooking Time:

Servings:

Ingredients:

- 1 chicken breast.
- 1 teaspoons of lemon juice
- 3 teaspoons of English sauce.
- White wine.
- 2 tbsp of butter
- ½ chicken cube
- 1 cup of water.

Directions:

1. Season the chicken with all the Ingredients B and brings it to the Air Fryer for 1015 minutes at 180ºC. Halfway through cooking check and flip. Make a sauce with the Ingredients that are left over.

2. It is Serve up with baked potatoes, yucca, or rice. It is accompanied by slices or vegetables.

Exquisite Bird Skewers

Prep Time:

Cooking Time:

Servings:

Ingredients:

- Chicken steaks
- Turkey fillets
- 1 cucumber
- Stalks of celery
- 2 cups of chimichurri
- ½ tomato tree
- 1 cup of carrot
- Sea salt

Directions:

1. Cut the steaks and marinate with chimichurri for 20 minutes. Place the pieces of meat on the skewers, alter nating with the vegetables, so that it is pleasing to the eye. Place in the Air Fryer for 1015 minutes at 200°C. Halfway through the cooking time, turn the skewers so that they cook evenly. Serve up by placing the skewers on the plate and in a small cup place the carrot paste.

2. Garnish with green leaves and sauce to taste.

Chicken Delight with Garlic

Prep Time:

Cooking Time:

Servings:

Ingredients:

- Chicken breast without skin.
- Olive oil
- 2 cloves of garlic
- 1/4 cup of Breadcrumbs.
- 1/4 cup grated Parmesan cheese
- Salt.

Directions:

1. Mix olive oil with crushed garlic and salt. Tap the breast and bathe with this mixture. In a separate bowl mix Parmesan cheese with breadcrumbs. Pass the chicken several times. Coat the mold of the fryer with oil and place the breast. Fry for 10 15 minutes at 160°C.

2. Flip and finish frying. Serve up with rice, vegetables or steamed potatoes.

Sensational Chicken

Prep Time:

Cooking Time:

Servings:

Ingredients:

- 1 chicken
- 2 onions
- 2 beers
- 1 Garlic head
- Thyme
- Salt and
- Pepper

Directions:

1. Chop the chicken in half. Give blows to soften the meat. Puncture it with a fork.

2. Finely chop the onion, crush the garlic, and add the other seasonings. Place them all in a bowl and dip the chicken, cover it and let it marinate overnight. The next morning, drain and take it to the Air Fryer for 1015 minutes at 180°c. Turn halfway through cooking and continue cooking.

Chicken Croquette

Prep Time:

Cooking Time:

Servings:

Ingredients:

- 2 parboiled chicken breasts.
- Garlic
- Carrot,
- Onion,
- Leek,
- Onion,
- Peppers
- Laurel.
- Ground bread
- 2 cups of wheat flour
- 4 scrambled eggs

Directions:

1. Crumble the breast, place in the processor with the other Ingredients and form a dough. Form the cro quettes and pass them through the beaten egg, then wheat flour.

2. Fry in Air Fryer for 610 minutes at 200°C. Check the cooking and flip.

9 781802 570557